LIFE
101

Colleen L. Reece
& Julie Reece

Linda, I pray God's richest blessings
on you as you graduate. Please accept
this little book of wisdom as a token
of your church's love.

A Barbour Book

June 11, 2000

LIFE
101

PART 1
LIFE'S LITTLE LESSONS

*Things they never told you you'd need to know
(or maybe you just weren't listening).*

*"Show me your ways,
O Lord,
teach me your paths;
guide me in your truth
and teach me,
for you are God
my Savior."*

Psalm 25: 4-5

Move on,
but Don't Slam the Door
Behind You

Jack breathed a sigh of relief on the last day of the part-time job he had held to help pay his way through college. His brand-new degree meant the opportunity for a more prestigious, higher-paying position.

"We can always use you," Jack's supervisor said. *No way will I be back,* Jack thought. He didn't want to be rude, so he just smiled—one of the wisest decisions of his life. He discovered jobs were scarce in his chosen field and the bills kept coming in. Part-time work at his former place of employment brought in a small, but steady paycheck until Jack found a job where he could better use his education and experience.

Life 101

Smile at little kids in grocery carts.
Once upon a time, you were one of them.

Make your bed when you get up,
so if you have visitors,
you won't have to make excuses.

Exercise the first thing in the morning.
It will get you going and you won't have to
worry about it the rest of the day.

If your clothes aren't dirty when you take them
off, hang them up so they won't pile up.

Treat your body well now.
The things you do
or don't do today
will affect you
for the rest of your life.

To Cut Down on Your Electrical Bill:

✓ Keep your refrigerator full. Use milk cartons or plastic jugs filled with water, if necessary.

✓ When you'll be gone more than a few days, turn off your hot water heater.

✓ Keep your car well-maintained. Changing the oil, filling the tires regularly and attending to minor repairs will save you dollars in the long run.

✓ Keep emergency kits for disasters in your car and your residence. Include in each:

> First aid kit
> Flashlight
> Extra batteries
> Nonperishable food to last two weeks
> Bottled water
> Prescription drugs
> Matches
> Small change
> Small bills
> Warm blanket(s)

Life 101

All About Food

✓ Turn pickle and mustard jars, etc. upside down in hot water to loosen caps.

✓ Toss a couple of soda crackers in your brown and granulated white sugar containers to keep the sugar from hardening.

✓ Plan to cook your meals backwards—write down how long it will take each item to cook.

✓ Remember: two items do *not* usually cook well together in the oven. Figure out when to begin preparing each item to finish the meal on time.

✓ Tally on a piece of paper the number of cups, half cups, tablespoons, and so on listed in a recipe as you add them. If you're distracted while counting, you won't ruin your recipe.

✓ Break eggs into a separate dish before adding. It saves time picking out shells if you goof and saves expensive ingredients if it's a bad egg.

Picking Produce

✓ Ripe cantaloupe and honeydew melons smell sweet.

✓ A ripe pineapple is heavy.

✓ To ripen fruit more quickly, stick in a plastic bag with a ripe banana.

✓ To slow the ripening process of fruit, keep it in a cool place.

✓ Round onions are often stronger than oval ones.

✓ Add apples and bananas to fruit salad, and tomatoes to tossed salad at the last minute to prevent them from turning brown or soggy.

✓ Give potato and pasta salad time in the refrigerator to blend flavors.

✓ Never add dressing to tossed salad until just before serving.

Life 101

In Their Nikes

Kelly scrunched down in her folding wheelchair. "What kind of assignment is this, anyway? I've never felt so weird in my whole life."

Her friend Jenny laughed and stopped pushing Kelly down the crowded mall. "Have you already forgotten what Mrs. DuJardin said?"

"No." Kelly switched to a believable imitation of their Contemporary Living teacher's voice. " 'An Indian proverb says never to judge a man until you have walked a mile in his moccasins.' "

"Except Mrs. Du added that to be contemporary we could change it to 'never expect to really understand others until you walk in their Nikes,' " Jenny added. "Chill out, will you? We could have drawn Tom and Jeff's assignment. How would you like to take turns being blindfolded on the busiest street in town?"

Kelly shuddered at the thought. "Allison and Christine had to go to a poor neighborhood, hang out on a corner and talk with people."

Jenny laughed. "Yeah. Jeff told them to be sure and wear their Nikes. People who hang out on street corners may need to make a fast getaway."

The girls didn't laugh long. Having people avoid them as if they had some kind of disease, or glance at Kelly and look quickly away made her feel like a nonperson. "Do you think we ever do that?" she asked.

Jenny hesitated. "Maybe. I never want people to think I'm staring."

Things got worse.

And worse.

In a shoe store a smiling clerk inquired, "What happened to you?"

Kelly motioned for Jenny to wheel her away. "Of all the insensitive jerks! What if I were in this chair for keeps and got asked that? He should do this assignment and see how it feels when people make stupid remarks."

"That's probably why Mrs. Du gave us this walk-in-their-Nikes assignment, although you aren't walking and I won't be when it's my turn."

Kelly sighed. "Well, things can't get much worse." Wrong. When Jenny wheeled her into a large empty elevator, a man started to step inside. He glanced at Kelly, the wheelchair, and stopped. "Uh, there isn't room. I'll wait."

"There's plenty of room," Kelly snapped.

"No, that's okay. I don't want to crowd you." He backed out, avoiding making eye contact with Kelly.

"That's it!" She jumped from the wheelchair. "Get in, Jenny."

Her friend rolled her eyes. "I can hardly wait."

Kelly watched her closely. Jenny's face reflected

the same new feelings Kelly had experienced: humiliation, anger, helplessness to combat prejudice—or was it only thoughtlessness? The rest of the time she watched the crowds. A few people smiled. One or two said hi. The rest walked past, "unseeing, uncaring, embarrassed, or all of the above," Kelly exploded when their awful two-hour assignment ended. "I'd like to stand up in the middle of the mall and tell everyone that being in a wheelchair doesn't make you different from anyone else." She folded the wheelchair and slammed it into the trunk of her car.

"Think they'd listen?" Looking troubled, Jenny slid into the car.

Kelly followed, started the car, then switched off the motor. "Come on, Jenny. We're going back. I need a new pair of Nikes." She sighed. "There's a lot of miles to walk and it takes time to break shoes in."

Jenny didn't say a word. She just checked to see is she had money for her own new Nikes and followed her friend's determined footsteps back into the mall.

PART 2
STUDY
PARTNERS

The difference between pass and fail.

Life 101

*"How good and pleasant it is when
brothers live together in unity!"*
Psalm 133:1

*"Then make my joy complete by
being like-minded, having the same love,
being one in spirit and purpose.
Do nothing out of
selfish ambition or vain conceit,
but in humility consider others
better than yourselves."*
Philippians 2:2-3

*". . .be of good comfort, be of one mind,
live in peace; and the God of
love and peace shall be with you."*
2 Corinthians 13:11 KJV

Don't date anyone
who doesn't have
the qualities
you are looking for
in a marriage partner.

Live by the Rules

Before you make a move on your best friend's boyfriend or girlfriend, consider this:

✓ You'll lose at least one friend, maybe more.

✓ If you fail, you'll feel ridiculous.

✓ If the person is fickle enough to leave your friend, chances are he or she won't stay with you, either.

✓ Using underhanded means makes you a loser, even if you win.

Life 101

No Instant Answers

Kathy got in with the wrong crowd during high school, simply because she was so lonely. She involved herself in drugs, alcohol, and crime, feeling accepted by others who did the same. Eventually, she bottomed out, unable to stand what she'd become.

Kathy decided enough was enough. She had to break her bad habits and move on. When she tried to do this, she discovered she was more isolated than ever. She bitterly told her mother, "I thought when I started making good choices things would be better. They aren't. At least when I was doing all those things I had friends. Now I don't have anyone."

Her mother quietly said, "Kathy, you have the mistaken impression that you can go from a bad crowd to a good crowd overnight. It's just not going to happen. There are no instant answers. I promise you, if you hang on and continue to make good choices, people will start to see and like the new you. You'll make good friends who will value your new standards and you will never have to go through this again."

It wasn't easy and it took a long time, but with the help of God and her family, Kathy hung in there until she found friends, happiness, and freedom.

Living With Assigned Partners

*"A friend loveth at all times,
and a brother is born for adversity."*
PROVERBS 17:17 KJV

*"A man of many companions
may come to ruin,
but there is a friend who
sticks closer than a brother."*
PROVERBS 18:24

*"As iron sharpens iron,
so one man sharpens another."*
PROVERBS 27:17

". . .there is a friend who sticks closer than a brother." This could well have been written about roommates! The following stories offer practical help in learning how to live and get along with roommates, coworkers, family, in-laws, and so forth.

Set up rules
before you start
living with someone.

Driving Brian Crazy!

Brian couldn't look at his roommate without gritting his teeth. Dustin's habits and comments ranged from annoying to totally offensive. If Brian had to sit through one more meal watching Dustin chew his dinner with an open mouth, or explain to one more date that the dirty socks and dishes in the living room weren't his, he was going to strangle Dustin.

One day a sentence from something Brian read stuck in his mind. *If you serve someone, it will change your own attitude.* "The person who wrote that didn't have to smell Dustin's socks," Brian muttered. "But if I don't do something, I'll go nuts. I guess it can't do any harm."

He found a card, scribbled, "Hope you do well on your test," pinned it to Dustin's pillow (which he found in the midst of his roommate's dirty-clothes pile) and left for class.

Hours later Brian returned to the empty apartment. A plate of chocolate cookies and a "thinking of you" card lay on his bed.

Change came. Not so much in Dustin—although he did grow more pleasant and made an effort to keep the apartment livable—but mostly in Brian's perception. Several years later, he received a card from the roommate who had almost driven him crazy. It spoke of how important Brian's friendship was to Dustin. The note ended, "You touched my life in more ways than you will ever know. I just want to say, you would be proud of what I am today."

Brian stared at the message, thankful that he hadn't missed knowing Dustin simply because of his dirty socks *and* Brian's unwillingness to look for the good in his friend.

". . .pray for them
which despitefully use you. . ."
MATTHEW 5:44 KJV

One Person, Different Views

In his wonderful book *Man's Search for Meaning,* Viktor Frankl tells the story of Dr. J., scourge of one of the worst German death camps during World War II. Never had a man so evil walked the halls of horror. Whispers of his inhuman experiments floated through the camp and strong men shuddered like frightened children.

Years later a man came to Viktor Frankl's study. The conversation turned to Germany, the war, and the concentration camps. "Did you know Dr. J.?" the visitor asked.

Frankl nodded.

The other's face lighted. "We were in prison together. He showed himself to be the best comrade you can imagine! He gave consolation to everybody. He lived up to the highest conceivable moral standard. He was the best friend I ever met during my long years in prison!"

The incident caused Viktor Frankl to write words that reflect the depths of God's mercy: *Every human being has the freedom to change at any instant.*

> ". . .Man looks at the outward appearance,
> but the Lord looks at the heart."
> 1 Samuel 16:7

Life 101

Something in Common

Lindsay's professor turned from the chalkboard and said, "No matter how unlikely it seems, each of us has something in common with every other human being." When the disbelieving stares of his students showed they didn't agree, he told this story:

The professor often served on negotiating teams, but his most difficult experience came when he was part of a team involved in negotiating with a member of a white supremacy group. An African-American, the professor vainly tried to put aside his discomfort and find a common meeting ground; anything from which to start. It proved impossible. Throughout the luncheon meeting, the professor met only with resistance. An hour later, negotiations remained at an impasse.

The professor took out his wallet to pay the bill. The supremacist glimpsed a picture. "Are those your children?" he asked.

A hundred questions raced through the professor's mind. If he told him yes, would it mean endangering his family? He hesitated, but reluctantly nodded.

"These are *my* children," the other replied. He brought out his wallet and proudly showed pictures. The only thing they had in common provided a strong enough meeting ground for them to complete a successful negotiation.

Sequel: The Exception?

Although challenged by her professor's assertion and story, Lindsay felt exceptions to the rule existed —namely, Mark. He sought her out at every opportunity, bombarding her with his own beliefs. "You don't belong in college," he maintained. "No woman does. Women should be in the home instead of taking places men should have."

After a few attempts to defend herself, Lindsay simply avoided Mark whenever she could. She decided he was the big-gest jerk she had ever encountered. In spite of this, she couldn't forget what her professor had said. One day she made an effort to talk with Mark on a neutral subject. When he responded appropriately, she tried another. To her amazement, she discovered they did have things in common. Not a lot, but enough to prove the professor's point: each person does have something in common with everyone else.

Jesus said when speaking to His disciples:
"I no longer call you servants. . .
Instead, I have called you friends. . ."
JOHN 15:15

PART 3

SCHOOL
OF HARD KNOCKS

Learning from life's painful lessons.

When you get
to the end of your rope,
tie a knot and hang on.

Death by Embarrassment

Contrary to popular belief, no one ever died of embarrassment. Just ask Beth.

"I came close," she relates. "I'd waited forever for Rick to ask me out. He finally did. I had so many butterflies I couldn't eat dinner. I didn't want my stomach to growl, so I grabbed a huge spoonful of peanut butter and ate it before brushing my teeth."

She grimaces. "Mistake number one. Peanut butter and butterflies don't mix. I ended up burping like an overstuffed baby! Rick showed up and walked me to the Jeep. I managed to hold off until he put me in and shut the door, then I let it fly. What a relief! It rocked Rick's Jeep, but he didn't seem to notice."

Beth giggles. "Some relief. He slid in behind the wheel, glanced in the backseat and said, 'Ready, everyone?' "

"Everyone? I cringed. Rick hadn't told me we were double dating. It's funny now, but when it happened, I thought I'd die." Laughter spills over. "The only good thing was I felt so embarrassed I didn't burp again for a week."

"IF"

If you can keep your head when all about you
    Are losing theirs and blaming it on you;
If you can trust yourself when all men doubt you,
    But make allowance for their doubting too:
If you can wait and not be tired by waiting,
    Or, being lied about, don't deal in lies.
Or being hated don't give way to hating,
    And yet don't look too good, nor talk too wise.

If you can dream—and not make dreams your
    master;
If you can think—and not make thoughts
    your aim,
If you can meet with Triumph and Disaster
    And treat those two impostors just the same.
If you can bear to hear the truth you've spoken
    Twisted by knaves to make a trap for fools,
Or watch the things you gave your life to, broken,
    And stoop and build 'em up with worn-out
        tools.

If you can make one heap of all your winnings
    And risk it on one turn of pitch-and-toss,
And lose, and start again at your beginnings,
    And never breathe a word about your loss:
If you can force your heart and nerve and sinew
    To serve your turn long after they are gone,

Life 101

And so hold on when there is nothing in you
    Except the Will which says to them: "Hold
        on!"

If you can talk with crowds and keep your virtue,
    Or walk with Kings—nor lose the common
        touch,
If neither foes nor loving friends can hurt you,
    If all men count with you, but none too much:
If you can fill the unforgiving minute
    With sixty seconds' worth of distance run,
Yours is the Earth and everything that's in it,
    And—which is more—you'll be a Man, my
        son!

RUDYARD KIPLING _(1865-1936)_

Running away
versus
Breaking Away.

There's a time to break away from your family to attend college, get married, or pursue a dream. An 18-year-old with a great chance for an out-of-state job is a lot different from a 14-year-old who runs away because she thinks her brother gets all the attention. Ecclesiastes 3 says God has a time for everything. It's like a basketball game. Sometimes you race down the floor. Sometimes you pass or play defense. The coach calls the signals.

Off the court, you call your own plays. Seeking the guidance of the Holy Spirit can help you know those plays are not only right for you, but perfectly timed.

When you feel like running, consider the following.

✓ Put things in perspective. What seems horrible at 2:00A.M. seldom seems so bad the next morning.

✓ Run away if you must, but to the beach, a park, or the library—a quiet place where you can have a few hours to think.

✓ Temporary isolation. Wounded animals often

hole up in a cave or den, but only for a time. If they don't come out, they die. You can die physically, emotionally, or spiritually if you isolate yourself too long.

✓ Counseling or support groups. They really do help.

✓ You are important. What if you didn't exist? Picture your family and friends. How would their lives be different? God created you as a special person whose life will touch many others. He expects you to handle tough times with His help and He understands your pain. Remember: He gave His only Son so that we could be free from sin.

The next time
you feel like running,
make it a quick jog
around the block.
Then consider your options.
If you see no way out,
make sure you run in
the right direction:
toward God,
who is there
and waiting.

Psalm 91

He that dwelleth in the secret place of the most
High shall abide under the shadow of the
   Almighty.
I will say of the LORD, He is my refuge and my
   fortress: my God; in him will I trust.
Surely he shall deliver thee from the snare of the
   fowler, and from the noisome pestilence.
He shall cover thee with his feathers, and under
   his wings shalt thou trust: his truth shall be
   thy shield and buckler.
Thou shalt not be afraid for the terror by night;
   nor for the arrow that flieth by day;
Nor for the pestilence that walketh in darkness;
   nor for the destruction that wasteth at
   noonday.
A thousand shall fall at thy side, and ten thousand
   at thy right hand; but it shall not come
   nigh thee.
Only with thine eyes shalt thou behold and see the
   eward of the wicked.
Because thou hast made the LORD, which is my
   refuge, even the most High, thy habitation;
There shall no evil befall thee, neither shall any
   plague come nigh thy dwelling.
For he shall give his angels charge over thee, to
   keep thee in all thy ways.
They shall bear thee up in their hands, lest thou

dash thy foot against a stone.

Thou shalt tread upon the lion and adder: the young lion and the dragon shalt thou trample under feet.

Because he hath set his love upon me, therefore will I deliver him: I will set him on high, because he hath known my name.

He shall call upon me, and I will answer him:

I will be with him in trouble;

I will deliver him, and honour him.

With long life will I satisfy him, and shew him my salvation.

KJV

PART 4

READING,
WRITING,
ARITHMETIC

And you thought school was over!

What You Don't Use, You Lose

*"Study to show yourself
approved unto God. . ."*
2 TIMOTHY 2:15 (paraphrased)

*"My son, if thou wilt receive my words,
and hide my commandments with thee;
So that thou incline thine ear unto wisdom,
and apply thine heart to understanding;
Yea, if thou criest after knowledge,
and liftest up thy voice for understanding;
If thou seekest her as silver,
and searchest for her as for hid treasures;
Then shalt thou understand the fear
of the LORD, and find the knowledge of God.
For the LORD giveth wisdom:
out of his mouth cometh
knowledge and understanding."*
PROVERBS 2:1-6 KJV

*"And that ye study to be quiet, and to do
your own business, and to work with your own
hands, as we commanded you."*
1 THESSALONIANS 4:11 KJV

Reading

*The importance of continuing
to study and learn throughout life*

The older Bill grew, the more set in his ways he became. When he learned he would be working in a foreign country for several years, he scorned the idea of learning the language. "English is good enough for me," he proudly said.

Bill discovered he was wrong. A few months after he started his new job, he had a mild heart attack. A local physician gave him a prescription to carry with him, in case of another incident.

A week later, a sharp pain warned him. He grabbed the bottle from his pocket and tried to open it. It wouldn't budge. He turned and twisted the child-proof cap with weakening fingers, unable to read the directions for opening it written in another language. If a friend had not happened to drop by in time, Bill would have died—as much a victim of ignorance as of his medical problem.

Recommended Reading

*Books I Wish Someone Had Told Me
to Read a Long Time Ago*

Books that Inspire

The Bible

America
Charles Kuralt

Chicken Soup for the Soul
Jack Canfield and Mark Victor Hansen

Diary of Anne Frank

Five Centuries of Verse

God's Smuggler
Brother Andrew

In His Steps
Charles M. Sheldon

Leaves of Gold
edited by Clyde Francis Lytle

Life 101

Life's Little Instruction Book
H. Jackson Brown, Jr.

My Utmost for His Highest
Oswald Chambers

The Hiding Place
Corrie ten Boom

The Pursuit of Holiness
Jerry Bridges

Books that Make You Feel Good

*All I Ever Needed to Know
I Learned in Kindergarten*
Robert Fulghum

Green Eggs and Ham and
Are You My Mother?
Dr. Seuss

Anything by Shel Silverstein, especially
The Giving Tree

The Little Engine that Could
Watty Piper

Life 101

The Velveteen Rabbit
Margery Williams Bianco

Where the Wild Things Are
Maurice Sendak

Goodnight Moon
Margor Brown

I'll Love You Forever
N. & J. Wright

Anne of Green Gables Series
L. M. Montgomery

A Christmas Carol
Charles Dickens

Charlotte's Web
E. B. White

Books that Provide Insight and Direction

The Bible

Man's Search for Meaning
Viktor Frankl

Life 101

Poetry
by Maya Angelou

Wake Up and Smell the Coffee
Ann Landers

Hinds' Feet on High Places
Hannah Hurnard

The Pilgrim's Progress
John Bunyan

Knowing God
J. I. Packer

Mere Christianity
C. S. Lewis

Practical Guidance for
Living Everyday Life

The Bible

A General Legal Guide

A Simplified Guide to Tax Return Preparation

Life 101

Better Homes and Gardens'
Family Medical Guide

Consumer Reports (before buying anything)

Cookbooks—Betty Crocker;
Better Homes and Gardens

NADA Official Used Car Guide and
The Kelley Blue Book (before buying a car)

What Color Is Your Parachute?

The Book of Virtues
William Bennett

The Elements of Style
Strunk and White

God's Little Instruction Book

Newspapers

Grit

USA Today
The Wall Street Journal

Life 101

The New York Times

Magazines

Guideposts
inspirational

Reader's Digest
general interest

Shape
physical fitness

U.S. News and World Report
worldwide news coverage

Christianity Today

Writing

_Here's a road map to help you find
and get where you're going._

Fill in the blanks on the following pages as honestly as you can. No one will see your answers but you and God.

Go back in six months or a year and do the questions again. Compare the answers to see how you're doing.

" 'For I know the plans I have for you',
declares the Lord,
'plans to prosper you and not to harm you,
plans to give you hope and a future.' "
JEREMIAH 29:11

Life 101

Who am I? _____

_____

_____

_____

_____

_____

_____

_____

_____

_____

_____

_____

_____

_____

_____

_____

_____

_____

_____

_____

_____

_____

_____

_____

Whom do I want to become? _____

_____
_____
_____
_____
_____
_____
_____
_____
_____
_____
_____

Why?_____

_____
_____
_____
_____
_____
_____
_____
_____
_____

Life 101

What are the five most important things in my life today? _____

_____

_____

_____

_____

_____

_____

_____

_____

_____

_____

Why? _____

_____

_____

_____

_____

_____

_____

_____

_____

_____

What do I believe will be the most important things in my life? _____

_____

_____

_____

_____

_____

_____

_____

_____

_____

Why? _____

_____

_____

_____

_____

_____

_____

_____

_____

_____

Life 101

Where do I see myself in five years? _____

_____

_____

_____

_____

_____

_____

_____

_____

_____

_____

_____

Where do I see myself in twenty years? _____

_____

_____

_____

_____

_____

_____

_____

_____

_____

Where do I see myself in fifty years? _____
_____
_____
_____
_____
_____
_____
_____
_____
_____

How am I making the world a better place right
now?_____
_____
_____
_____
_____
_____
_____
_____
_____
_____

Life 101

How will I make the world a better place in the future? _____
_____
_____
_____
_____
_____
_____
_____
_____

When will I start? _____
_____
_____
_____
_____
_____
_____
_____
_____
_____

Arithmetic

Sometimes a broke student or new grad is forced to play a lot with numbers in the kitchen, such as:

✓ Trying to make something from nothing

✓ Wondering if a small package of noodles and a half-can of three-day-old soda will last a week

✓ Deciding if you can really chop one small candy bar into twenty pieces

✓ Or if one can of soup can be watered down enough to feed three friends whose cupboards make Old Mother Hubbard's look like a supermarket

✓ Trying to calculate whether you just added the third or fourth cup of flour

✓ Figuring out how to lose five pounds before a big date in two days

✓ Attempting to add an ingredient at the end of a recipe after forgetting it earlier

A Story of Sharing

*When you don't think you can stretch
the remnants of your food
through the end of the week,
remember what faith can do.*

"The people are hungry," the disciples told Jesus. "They have come to hear You but they have no food."

"There are five thousand men, plus women and children," one said. "What shall we do?"

Andrew, Simon Peter's brother, spoke, "There is a lad here, who has five barley loaves and two small fishes: but what are they among so many?"

"Make the men sit down," Jesus instructed. He took the boy's lunch, gave thanks, and distributed it to His wondering disciples. They in turn gave it to the people, scarcely believing their eyes when more and more kept coming. When all had eaten, twelve baskets yet remained. John 6:1-14 (paraphrased.)

Another. . .

Remember the wonderful old French folk tale, "Stone Soup?" Two strangers came to a hamlet where people were hoarding food for fear of starvation. They persuaded the villagers to bring what they had and put it together in one large kettle. One by one the poor people each brought a small offering:

    a carrot or two
    a small potato
    a handful of beans

The magic that turned their offerings into "stone soup" and fed the entire village was not the ordinary rock the strangers dropped in, but the spirit of sharing.

If there's too much month at the end of your money and your refrigerator is perilously close to empty, call a few friends. Invite them to bring anything they have on hand and make a luck-of-the-pot meal. You may end up with a strange menu, but you'll have fun—and something to eat!

Life 101

Numerical Quips

✓ God + one = a majority.

✓ Everyone is equal in God's eyes.

✓ In marriage, one + one = one.

✓ Spending more money than you earn just doesn't add up.

✓ It's hard to erase first impressions.

✓ Second thoughts are often best.

✓ A little humor in any equation makes things work out better.

✓ If you haven't tried three different ways to accomplish the same thing, don't give up.

✓ Following the Ten Commandments adds up to hundreds of blessings.

✓ A "paycheck" in the hand is worth two in the bush.

✓ If you put God first and others second, you will find happiness.

✓ Spending effort and energy today = success tomorrow.

✓ Budget: a plan for systematically going broke.

✓ Quarterback: a nominal refund.

✓ Bank: a place where you can borrow money provided you can prove you don't need to.

✓ It's easy for anyone to meet expenses. You find them everywhere.

✓ The cost of living doesn't seem to affect its popularity.

PART 5
SUNDAY SCHOOL LESSONS

Spiritual guidance for every day of the week.

Day 1: From Grief to Hope

*"Weeping may endure for a night,
but joy cometh in the morning."*
PSALM 30:5 KJV

Mary and her sister Martha anxiously waited for Jesus to come. Surely He would heal their brother, whom He loved, when He had healed so many others! Jesus did not come and Lazarus died. The sisters sadly prepared him for burial, hot tears falling on the linen wrappings. They laid him to rest in a cave, rolled a stone before it, and the household went into mourning.

"Jesus could have saved Lazarus," Martha said.

"I know." Her sister sighed, eyes filled with sadness.

Four days later Jesus came. Mary and Martha cried, "Lord, if You had been here, our brother would not have died!"

Jesus wept. Then he ordered that the stone be taken from the mouth of the cave. He looked toward heaven and prayed, "Father, I thank You that You have heard me." In a loud voice, he cried, "Lazarus, come forth!"

Torn between grief and hope, the sisters could hardly force themselves to look. A moment later they fell to their knees. Their brother stood before them, alive and smiling. (Based on John 11.)

Even when things
seem the darkest,
we can be hopeful Christ
will make them better soon.

Day 2: From Guilt to Forgiveness

*"Though your sins are like scarlet,
they shall be as white as snow."*
ISAIAH 1:18

"Master, this woman was taken in adultery. Moses has commanded us that such should be stoned. What do you say?"

The accused woman cringed, her whole miserable life flashing before her. She waited for Jesus to give His assent. Instead, He stooped down. She saw Him write on the ground with his finger. Was it her death sentence?

The crowd demanded that Jesus reply. He said, "He that is without sin among you, let him first cast a stone at her."

The woman scarcely dared breathe. She waited for the first sharp stone to tear her flesh. None came. She looked up. The crowd had silently stolen away.

At last, Jesus arose and asked, "Woman, where are your accusers? Has no man condemned you?"

Trembling, she stammered, "No man, Lord."

He looked into her eyes. "Neither do I condemn you: go, and sin no more." She stumbled away, weeping hot, healing tears that washed away her guilt and set her free. (Based on John 8.)

No matter what
you have done,
or how terrible your sin,
the Lord will forgive you
if you'll only repent
and come to Him.

Day 3:
From Selflessness to Reward

*"May the Lord repay you for what you have done.
May you be richly rewarded by the Lord. . . ."*
RUTH 2:12

Soon after Solomon was crowned king, two women came to him with babies, one dead, one living. The first said, "O King, we were sleeping with our children in one bed. This woman lay on her child in her sleep and it died. She put it beside me while I slept, took my baby, and said it was hers."

"She speaks falsely!" the other denied. "She is the mother of the dead child."

Solomon considered the problem for a long time. Then he said to a guard, "Take a sword, divide the living child, and give half to each woman."

One of the women said, "Yes. Cut the child in two and divide it between us." The other fell to her knees before the throne and cried out, "No, do not kill my son! Give the baby to her, but let him live."

Solomon ruled, "Give the child to the woman who would not have it slain. She is the real mother."

The woman who had been willing to give up her baby in order that he might live held the child close to her bosom and wept tears of joy. (Based on 1 Kings 3.)

Putting the interests
of others ahead of our own
brings great blessings.

Day 4: From Fear to Peace

"And the peace of God,
which passeth all understanding,
shall keep your hearts and minds
through Christ Jesus."
Philippians 4:7 KJV

Jesus knelt alone in the orchard of olive trees known as the Garden of Gethsemane. Peter, James, and John waited a little distance away, so weary they could not watch with Him even one hour. Soon Judas Iscariot would come with a band of men to seize Him. Now was the time to prepare for what lay ahead.

Great drops of sweat like blood fell to the earth. Groans wracked His tortured body and mind. One disciple had betrayed Him. Another would deny Him before the cock crowed in the morning. All would run away. Had those who followed learned so little in the weeks and months during which He had tried to teach them? The Son of God was also Son of man. The human side of Jesus shuddered. If only He could face death knowing His mission had not failed. Could those He had chosen carry on the work He had barely begun? Or would His sacrifice be for nothing?

"Father," He cried. "If it be possible, let this cup pass away from me. Nevertheless, not as I will, but as You will!" No sign came that God's plan would be altered. He bowed his head, so drained by the struggle, it felt as if life had flown, leaving only an empty shell.

Just when Jesus knew He could bear no more, an angel came from heaven and ministered to Him. A surge of peace flowed through Jesus.

Even though He watched his disciples vanish into the night, Jesus no longer feared. Weak and human as they were, in a short time their eyes would be opened. They would understand many things and serve Him until their deaths.

Heart and mind at peace, Jesus silently allowed his captors to lead him toward the high priest's house. (Based on Matthew 26; Luke 22.)

No matter how frightened or scared we are,
we can always find the peace that passes understanding through Jesus Christ.

Day 5: From Weakness to Strength

"I can do everything through him
who gives me strength."
PHILIPPIANS 4:13

Esther stood trembling outside the royal court. Dared she enter without invitation? If her husband, King Ahasuerus, did not hold out his golden scepter in welcome, she would be put to death. He had already banished Vashti, his former queen, for refusing to come at his command and show off her beauty to his drunken guests. What might he do to Esther for asking him to lift the death decree he had issued against the Jews?

"I cannot let my people be slaughtered," she whispered. "I am also Jewish. Should it be discovered, I will be subject to death. Besides, my people are counting on me." She gathered her royal robes about her and went into the inner court, heart pounding like the thunder of many chariots going to war.

When the king saw her, he held out the golden scepter and offered whatever she requested, up to half of his kingdom. Weak with relief, Esther invited him to a banquet, where she exposed the evil plotting of wicked Haman and saved her people from extermination. (Based on the Book of Esther.)

Even when we feel
too weak to meet
tomorrow's challenges,
we can ask for
and receive strength
from God.

Day 6: From Oppression to Freedom

"Trust in the LORD with all thine heart;
and lean not unto thine own understanding.
In all thy ways acknowledge him,
and he shall direct thy paths."
PROVERBS 3:5-6 KJV

Longer than many could remember, the children of Israel had been trapped in bondage by the Egyptians, who had made slaves of them.

At first they had clung to the promise of a Deliverer, one who would lead them out of captivity. Yet as month after month dragged into long years of poverty, misery, and trouble, even that single ray of light in a dark world flickered low. "How long, O Lord?" the people cried out in despair.

God heard those cries. He saved Moses from Pharaoh's order that all boy babies born among the Jewish people must be killed and molded Moses to be a leader of the Israelites.

After many years of pleading and a series of terrible plagues, Pharaoh allowed Moses to lead the Exodus to the Promised Land. Gone were the people's hopelessness and helplessness. God Himself had freed them from oppression. (Based on Exodus 1-12.)

Patience and faith
in the most difficult
circumstances
will be rewarded.

Day 7:
From Anger to Understanding

"Love your enemies and pray for those who persecute you. . ." MATTHEW 5:44

Simon Peter had never felt more miserable. How could Jesus allow this? Anger and hurt lay like stones in Peter's heart. His eyes flashed. "Even though all shall be offended, I will not," he declared. There! Now Jesus would know whatever happened, at least one would be beside Him. Jesus responded, "Peter, before the cock crows twice, you will deny me three times."

"If I should die with you, I will not deny you," he shouted. The others agreed.

A few hours later, Peter stared with consternation at Jesus. Had he not defended the Master by cutting off an enemy's ear with his own sword? Now it was back on the man's head as if it had never been severed! Why had Jesus healed one of those who came to take Him? Peter fled, confused and angry. By the second crowing of the cock the next morning, he had indeed denied Jesus three times.

Not until after Jesus' resurrection, did Peter begin to understand who and what Jesus really was. When he did, he gladly faced persecution, prison, and death rather than deny the Master. (Based on the Gospels of Matthew, Mark, Luke, and John.)

Placing yourself in another's
shoes often turns anger to
understanding.

Alone

"Be still and know that I am God."
PSALM 46:10

One of the lowest times I ever experienced came just after I began my first year of law school. I had to leave for college, several states away, the morning after my grandmother's memorial service. I missed her an awful lot. Grandma was a friend who believed in me, listened, and understood.

One evening, I dragged home from classes. I looked at the stars, wishing Grandma were there with me. Being the youngest member of the law school meant competing with those much older and more experienced. How could I concentrate on increasingly difficult studies when I felt so alone and sad?

I thought of Grandma's memorial service and the friends and family who had been there. My mind focused on Marian, a victim of several disabling illnesses.

Marian arrived in a wheelchair. She had spent hours during the final, hard days with my aunt who lived with and cared for Grandma. After the service, my sister and I talked with Marian.

She told us, "Right now everyone is giving your aunt the support she needs: flowers, cards, time. I'm going to wait and watch these next few months.

There will be times when Colleen will need love and support and won't be able to let people know how much she is hurting. I'll give my flowers then."

How nice it would be to have someone like Marian right then: watching to make sure I was okay; ready to lend a listening ear; able to recognize things weren't all right ·without my having to say anything.

Through my own dark thoughts, I felt a small light. I already had Someone. He had been with me all along. He knew when things were the darkest in my life, without my having to say a word. He knew when I needed a flower, or a card, or a listening ear. I realized no matter how far away I was from my family, no matter how hard, discouraging, or lonely the road I walked, He would always be there for me.

Jesus is also called Emmanuel, which means *"God with us."*

Hundreds of years ago Moses told the people, *"The Lord. . .will be with you; he will never leave you nor forsake you. . ."* (Deuteronomy 31:8).

It's just as true now as it was then.

Psalm 23

The Lord is my shepherd; I shall not want.
He maketh me to lie down in green pastures:
He leadeth me beside the still waters.
He restoreth my soul:
He leadeth me in the paths of righteousness
    for his name's sake.
Yea, though I walk through the valley
    of the shadow of death,
I will fear no evil: for thou art with me;
Thy rod and thy staff they comfort me.
Thou preparest a table before me in the presence
    of mine enemies:
Thou anointest my head with oil;
    my cup runneth over.
Surely goodness and mercy shall follow me all
    the days of my life:
And I will dwell in the house of the LORD for ever.

KJV

PART 6:
CLIFF NOTES

*Before Jesus reached the mountain
where He taught and helped others,
He had to climb.*

So do we!

Bare Necessities
to Help You
Keep Climbing

✓ Life is not so much a destination as a journey.

✓ Start and end every day by giving your heavenly Father a "Thank You" for simply being alive.

✓ The way we choose to walk determines where we will end up.

✓ You will never fall as far if you're connected to a friend.

✓There is always Someone who understands exactly how we feel.

✓ It's easier to recognize and avoid pitfalls by talking with someone who has already traveled that road.

✓ Jesus walked every path, felt every feeling, and overcame every obstacle we will ever have to face.

✓ When two walk together, the road never seems so long.

We don't have to
walk alone.
Jesus is with us,
if we invite Him to come.

*"And I will walk among you,
and will be your God,
and ye shall be my people."*
Leviticus 26:12 KJV

Others Who Will
Often Walk with Us
if only We Ask

✓ a dad, mom, or stepparent

✓ a sister or brother

✓ a relative outside the immediate family

✓ a neighbor

✓ a special friend

✓ a pastor, teacher, counselor, or doctor

✓ Most importantly, remember that you have a Friend in Jesus. You can always turn to Him in prayer.

> _"My voice shalt thou hear_
> _in the morning, O LORD;_
> _in the morning will I direct_
> _my prayer unto thee, and will look up."_
> **Psalm 5:3 KJV**

Life 101

We All Need Shelters
Along the Way;
Places to Go When
Life's Storms Rage

✓ Karen heads for the spare bedroom at a friend's house.

✓ Dave goes fishing in a pool as deep as his thoughts.

✓ Lorie "visits old friends" by rereading a beloved childhood book.

✓ Ken digs out a familiar Disney video or a musical.

✓ Jodi and Carol make "comfort food": mashed potatoes, pudding, and so on.

✓ Jennifer curls up with her favorite stuffed animal and listens to music.

✓ Michael turns off his answering machine.

✓ Wendy takes a long, hot bubble bath.

✓ Brinn drives with the radio turned up.

✓ Allison goes shopping.

✓ Tim goes for a long walk.

✓ Brent and Christine go hiking in the mountains.

Life 101

Worth Remembering

✓ After six months, a good reputation will get you farther than anything on your resume.

✓ "I'm sorry" and "I goofed" make more friends than any explanation will.

✓ Always write down the name (first and last), position, telephone number, date, time you talk with someone. Keep it in a file.

✓ Buy a calendar at the beginning of the year. Write in important birthdays, anniversaries, and holidays. Make a note a week before each event to send a card.

✓ On Mother's or Father's Day, Valentine's Day, Christmas, or birthdays, take time to write cards and tell people how much they mean to you.

✓ Once a month, write a letter to someone who has changed your life for the better, and tell them.

✓ There is no one you will ever meet who cannot do something better or see something more clearly than you can. Ask yourself every time you meet someone new, "What can I learn from this person?"

✓ Youth comes but once in a lifetime, according to Henry Wadsworth Longfellow. Perhaps, but it remains strong in many for their entire lives.

✓ Recycle and treat the earth with respect. It may be the only legacy you leave to future generations.

✓ Spend more time with friends and family. You will never regret it.

Story from a Far Country

"My father, I am sad today," a brown-skinned boy told a wise village man.

The old man looked at him. "Sad? This is a day of harvest and thanksgiving. We bring offerings to God, to be used by our chief for those in need."

The boy bowed his head. "That is why I am so sad. Father and Mother are so poor they can spare but a few vegetables. I have nothing to give."

The old man smiled. "You have something more precious than you know, my son. None but you can give it."

That afternoon, members of the tribe silently laid their offerings on a blanket before the chief: A bowl of grain. Squash. A handwoven basket or rug. Each time the chief nodded, then raised his hands and blessed the giver.

The boy came last. He lay down on the blanket. "I have nothing to give except myself." The chief raised his hands in blessing—and the old man smiled.

_"For whosoever will save his life shall lose it;
but whosoever shall lose his life for my sake
and the gospel's, the same shall save it.
For what shall it profit a man,
if he shall gain the whole world,
and lose his own soul?"_
MARK 8:35-36 KJV

Giants and Dwarfs

A man who lived in a small town contemplatively walked home after a heated church discussion on who would be greatest in the kingdom of heaven. "Works." "Saved." "Financial support." "Humble like a child." "Well-versed in Scripture." Such words and phrases tripped through his mind. What did they mean? How did God truly measure greatness?

That night the man had a dream. He saw a huge mirror set up in the downtown square. Unlike other mirrors, it reflected the inside of people, not the outside!

As everyone in town gathered in the park, an angel appeared by the mirror. "Today we will learn which of you truly loves and serves God," the angel said. "When each of you steps before the mirror I will record what it shows." He held up a book containing the name of every person in town.

"Who will be first?" the angel asked.

The mayor stepped forward; a tall man, everlastingly busy with city affairs. "It is right and fitting that I be first," he announced importantly.

"Very well. Stand here, please."

The smiling mayor strode toward the mirror. A gasp went through the crowd, for the closer he got to the measuring mirror, the smaller his image grew. When he reached the mirror, his reflection had shrunk until he looked like a tiny dwarf! How could such a thing happen? Everyone thought the mayor was so good.

"I don't understand!" he blustered. "Surely there is some kind of mistake."

"The mirror shows the truth," the keeper of the mirror quietly said to the startled people. "Who will be next?"

No one dared stand before a mirror that turned a mayor into a dwarf. At last the keeper of the mirror called a name. The crowd buzzed. The small man lived in a tiny house on a run-down street and mended shoes for a living. What kind of image could he cast? Yet no one dared disobey the angel.

The cobbler timidly came forward. The crowd not only gasped, they cried out in amazement. When the man reached the mirror, a giant image appeared, so enormous it wouldn't even fit inside the frame!

"How can this be?" the mayor roared in humiliation.

The angel smiled. "The mirror knows this man's heart."

One by one, the people came forward. Many of those considered important by the townspeople cast only dwarflike shadows. Only a few reflected giant images. The young female doctor who never refused to treat those who could not pay. The widow who faithfully taught a class of rebellious Sunday school boys. A teenager who helped Meals on Wheels. A child who eagerly ran forward and clapped chubby hands when he saw himself be-come a giant in the mirror.

Finally, only the man who was dreaming remained.

The keeper of the mirror beckoned to him. "Come. It is your turn."

The man slowly walked toward him, dragging his feet. If those held in such high esteem only cast a dwarf's shadow, he might not cast a shadow at all.

Before he reached the measuring mirror, the man awakened. A river of relief ran through him. It had only been a dream. He slipped from bed and knelt, asking God's help—not to become the best, only his best. For the rest of his life, he remembered the dream and became a true giant in service to God and others.

*"Then the righteous will answer [the King],
'Lord, when did we see you hungry and feed you,
or thirsty and give you something to drink?
When did we see you a stranger and invite you
in, or needing clothes and clothe you?
When did we see you sick or in prison
and go to visit you?'
The King will reply, 'I tell you the truth,
whatever you did for one of the least of
these brothers of mine, you did for me.'"*
MATTHEW 25:37-40

Life 101

The Race

An unknown author tells the story of a race. Trembling with fear, hope, and excitement, young children line up. Their parents watch from the sidelines, cheering for their kids.

The whistle blows and off they go! A boy near the lead thinks how proud his dad must be. The next moment, he slips and falls. "Quit! Give up, you're beaten!" the crowd jeers. For a moment, he believes it. Then the fallen boy sees his father's face. He can almost hear his dad shout, "Get up and win the race!"

He leaps to his feet and races on, only to fall a second time, a third! Three strikes and you're out. Why go on? Yet his father's voice rings in his ears. "Get up and win the race!"

The boy springs to his feet. He cannot win but he will not quit. He hears the cheers for the winner and keeps on running. Head bowed, he comes in last, to louder cheers than the winner received. "I didn't do well," he sadly tells his father. His wonderful dad says, "To me you won. Each time you fell, you rose."

The boy becomes a man. He faces dark, hard times. Always the memory of that little boy helps him know that all you have to do to win is to keep on getting up and going on. "Quit! Give up, you're beaten," people still shout in his face. But his father's voice rings in his ears, "Get up and win the race!"

Tomorrow

Beyond the shadows of a far distant shore;
The promises of tomorrow lie untouched in the
    mist,
Not quite reality—then again, much more,
Providing the reasons we exist.
The traces of days left behind grow silent, cease
    their whisperings.
Only faint memories remind of the joys and
    sorrows life brings.
With gaze ahead and heart behind, we lose the
    path on which we tread,
So intent we are to find the path that lies ahead.
And when the distant shore is reached,
When the day draws to a close,
The mists will lift and we will see
The joys of life were the paths we chose.

Dare to listen and learn
what God is asking of you,
enjoy every step of your life,
and always remember:
God never gives us
tests that are too hard
for us to pass.

"And God is faithful;
he will not let you be tempted beyond
what you can bear.
But when you are tempted,
he will also provide a way out
so that you can stand up under it."
1 Corinthians 10:13 KJV

Inspirational Library

Beautiful purse/pocket size editions of Christian classics bound in flexible leatherette. These books make thoughtful gifts for everyone on your list, including yourself!

The Bible Promise Book　　Over 1000 promises from God's Word arranged by topic. What does God promise about matters like: Anger, Illness, Jealousy, Love, Money, Old Age, and Mercy? Find out in this book!
　　Flexible Leatherette $3.97

Daily Light　　One of the most popular daily devotionals with readings for both morning and evening.
　　Flexible Leatherette $4.97

Wisdom from the Bible　　Daily thoughts from Proverbs which communicate truths about ourselves and the world around us.
　　Flexible Leatherette $4.97

My Daily Prayer Journal　　Each page is dated and features a Scripture verse and ample room for you to record your thoughts, prayers, and praises. One page for each day of the year.
　　Flexible Leatherette $4.97